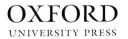

OXFORD
UNIVERSITY PRESS

Is This too Much?

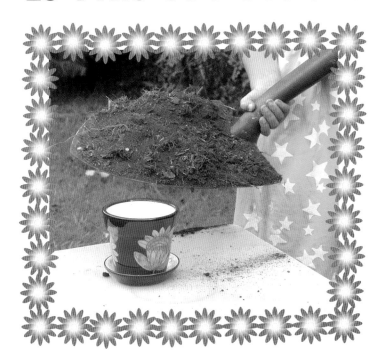

Lesley Pether

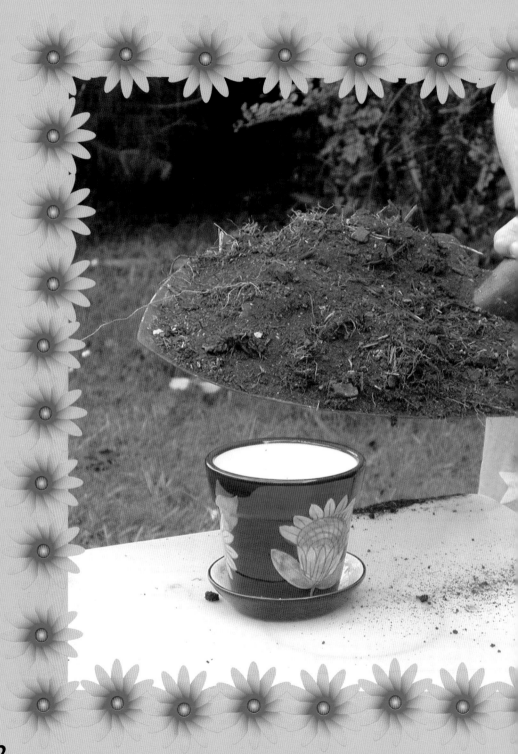

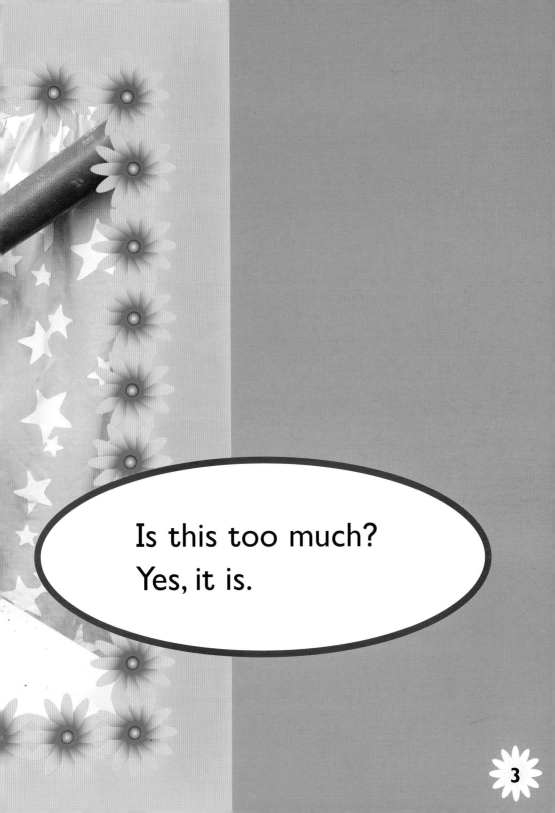

Is this too much?
Yes, it is.

3

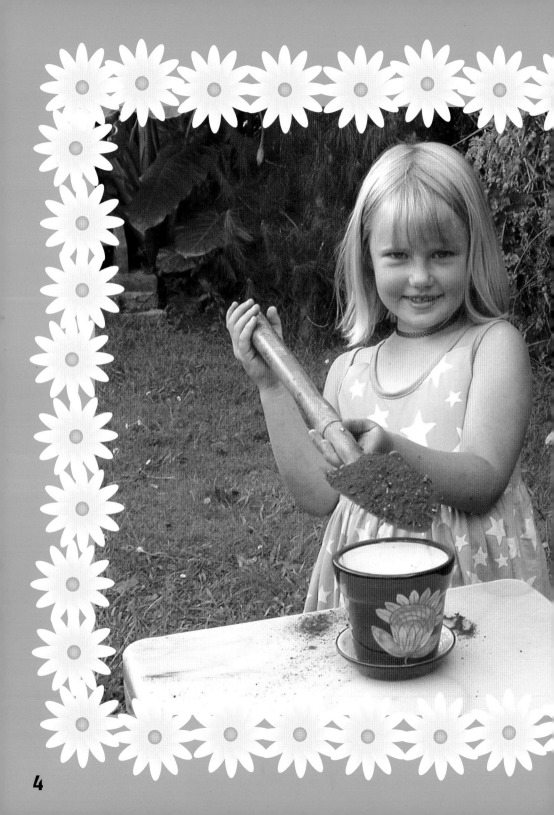

Is this too much?
No, it is not.

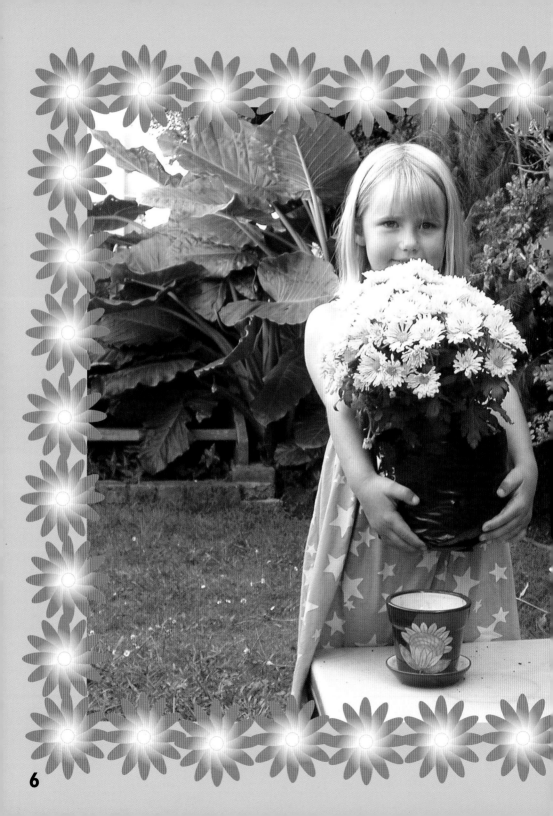

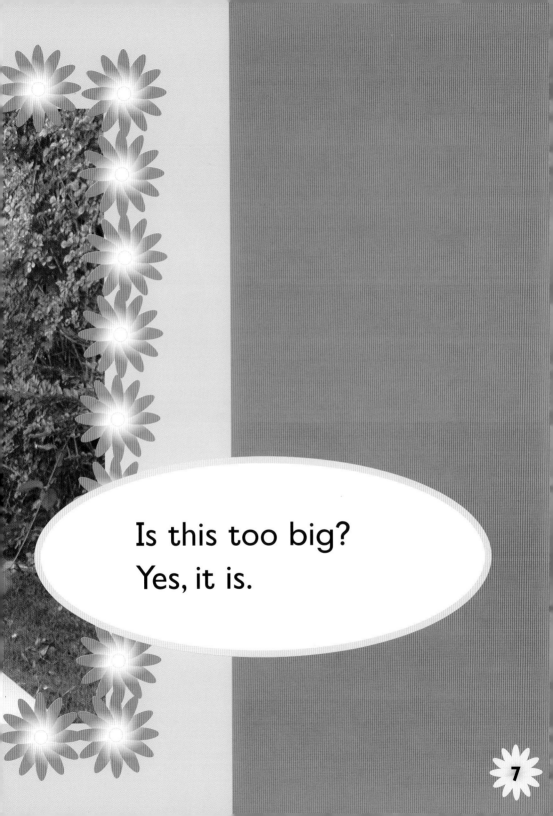

Is this too big?
Yes, it is.

7

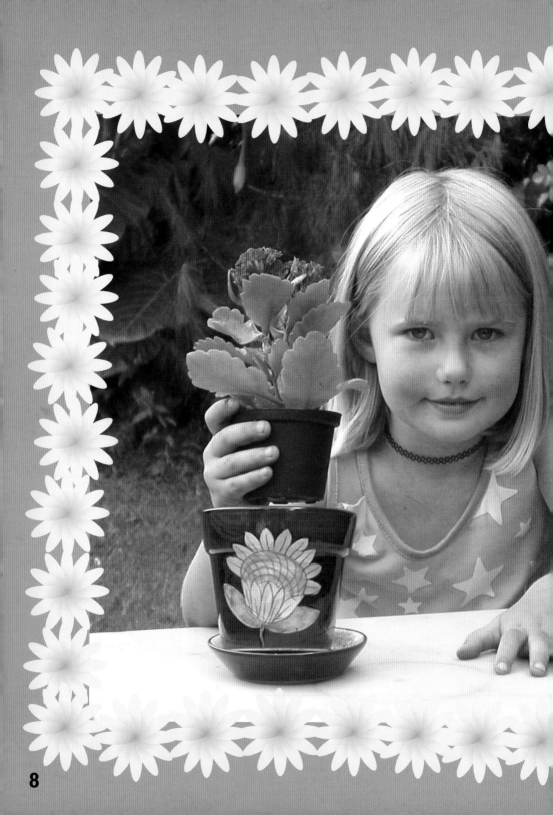

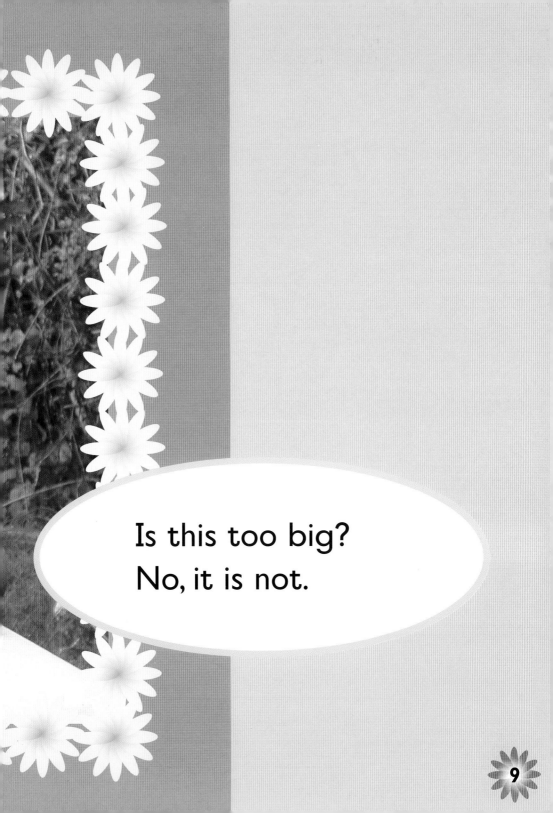

Is this too big?
No, it is not.

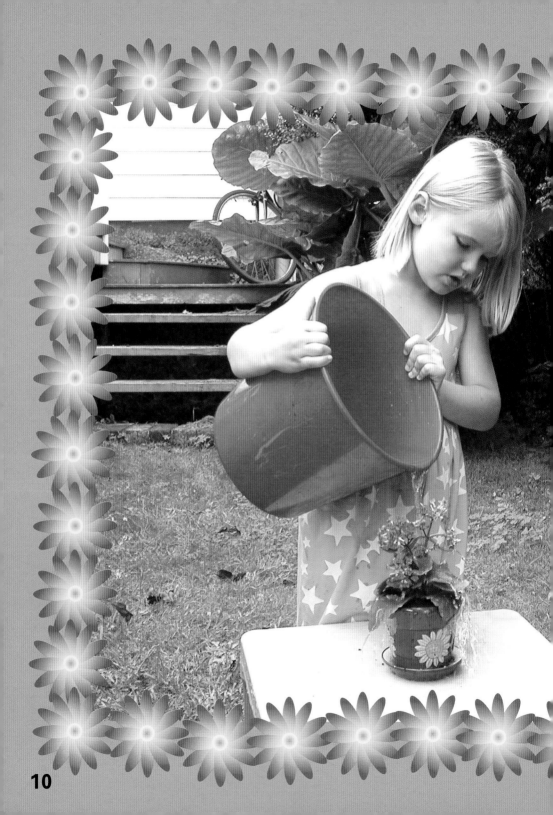

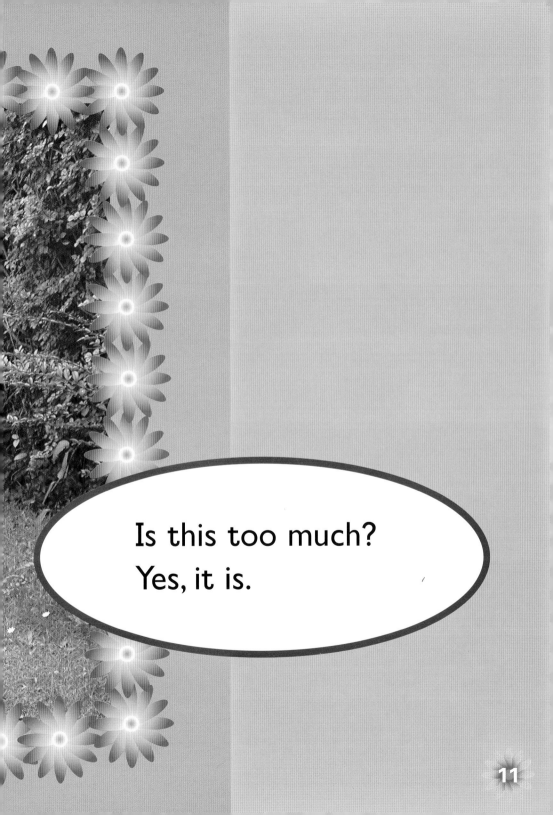

Is this too much?
Yes, it is.

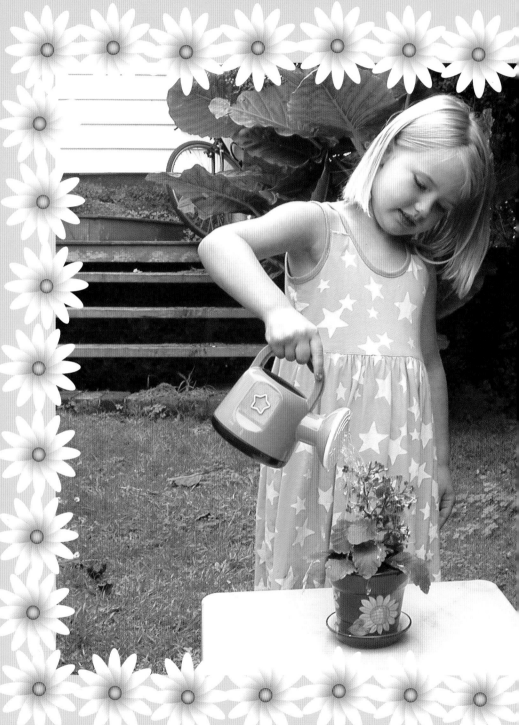

Is this too much?
No, it is not.

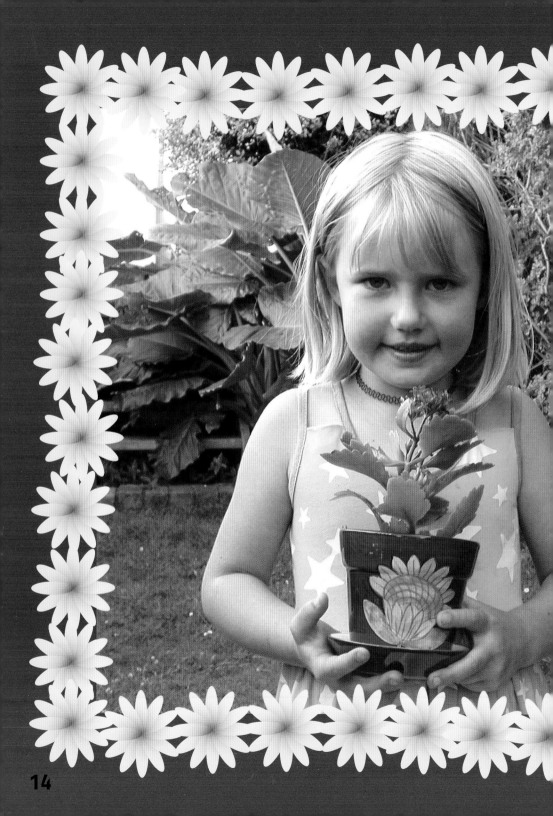

14

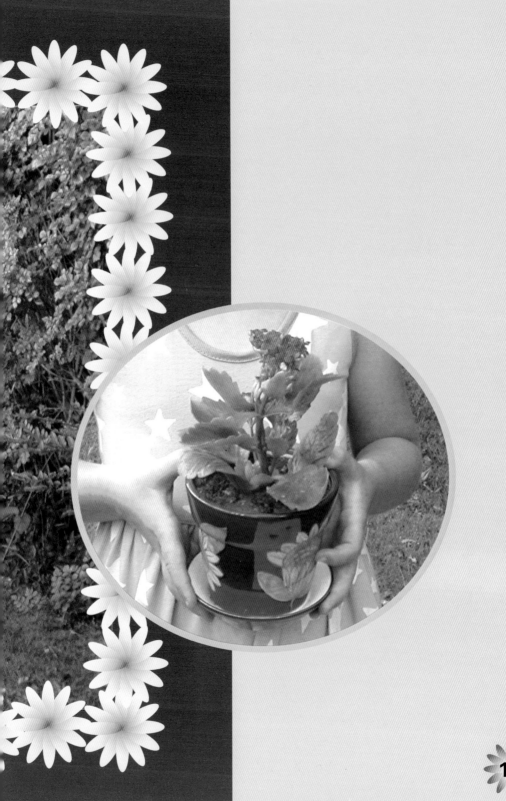

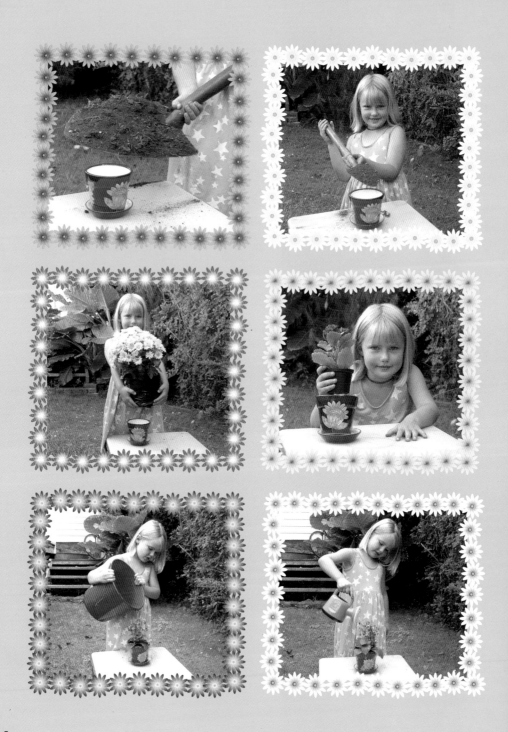